fast & simple
100 everyday recipes

First published in 2011
LOVE FOOD is an imprint of Parragon Books Ltd

Parragon
Chartist House
15-17 Trim Street
Bath BA1 1HA, UK
www.parragon.com

ISBN: 978-1-4454-4712-4

Printed in China

Produced by Ivy Contract
Cover photography by Mike Cooper
Cover image home economy and food styling by Lincoln Jefferson

Notes for the Reader

This book uses both metric and imperial measurements. Follow the same units of measurement throughout; do not mix metric and imperial. All spoon measurements are level: teaspoons are assumed to be 5 ml, and tablespoons are assumed to be 15 ml. Unless otherwise stated, milk is assumed to be full fat, eggs and individual vegetables are medium, and pepper is freshly ground black pepper.

The times given are an approximate guide only. Preparation times differ according to the techniques used by different people and the cooking times may also vary from those given. Optional ingredients, variations or serving suggestions have not been included in the calculations.

Recipes using raw or very lightly cooked eggs should be avoided by infants, the elderly, pregnant women, convalescents and anyone suffering from an illness. Pregnant and breastfeeding women are advised to avoid eating peanuts and peanut products. Sufferers from nut allergies should be aware that some of the ready-made ingredients used in the recipes in this book may contain nuts. Always check the packaging before use.

Vegetarians should be aware that some of the ready-made ingredients used in the recipes in this book may contain animal products. Always check the packaging before use.

fast & simple

introduction

If you don't have the time or the inclination to spend a lot of time in the kitchen, but enjoy fresh, tasty wholesome food and creative cooking, then these recipes are for you. Many of the recipes take ten minutes or less to cook, excluding preparation time. They are full of flavour and goodness, but take little time and effort to prepare, as the food is prepared and cooked very quickly.

Convenience foods and ready meals are expensive, often boring and usually have a bland or artificial flavour designed to appeal to a mass market. More importantly they are frequently loaded with preservatives to give them a longer shelf life. But 'fast' food doesn't have to mean a cocktail of nasty chemicals. You can cook fresh foods quickly with the minimum of fuss but maximum flavour and, of course, you'll know exactly what has gone into them.

The keys to success are using top quality foods; always choose the freshest and best quality produce for optimum flavour, such as free-range eggs, vibrant fruit and vegetables free from blemishes and bruises, fresh herbs, extra virgin olive oil, etc. A well stocked storecupboard and good utensils make cooking much

easier. Basic staples should include rice and pasta. Both fresh and dried pasta are produced in a variety of shapes and sizes, and cook in minutes. Good seasoning is particularly important when food is cooked for a short time, so a stock of good wine vinegar, honey, spices, herbs and sauces, such as Tabasco and Worcestershire, are invaluable to use in recipes to add interest and variety. Canned fish (sardines, anchovies, tuna), tomatoes, sweetcorn and beans are also excellent to keep in the cupboard and you can use these old favourites to add a new imaginative twist to recipes. Cream and yogurt are wonderfully versatile ingredients, perfect for pouring, whipping and spooning, and will add a smooth richness to both sweet and savoury dishes. In the freezer, ready rolled pastry and good quality ice cream are ideal standbys.

There's no fiddly preparation in any of these recipes – just simple, tasty food that looks and tastes fabulous. There really is nothing better or more delicious than making your own meals, so try these trouble-free, straightforward recipes and taste the difference.

under 10 minutes

garden pea soup

ingredients

serves 1

600 ml/1 pint vegetable stock
450 g/1 lb fresh or frozen peas
pinch of granulated sugar
125 ml/4 fl oz single cream
salt and pepper
2 tbsp single cream, to garnish
crusty rolls, to serve

method

1 Bring the stock to the boil in a large saucepan. Add the peas and cook for 5 minutes.

2 Remove the pan from the heat, season with sugar, and salt and pepper, then transfer to a food processor or blender and process until smooth.

3 Pour into a saucepan, stir in the cream and heat gently to simmering point.

4 Taste and adjust the seasoning if necessary, then pour into 4 serving bowls, adding a swirl of single cream to each bowl. Serve with crusty rolls.

chilled avocado soup

ingredients

serves 6

4 ripe avocados, halved,
    stoned and peeled
1 garlic clove
1.2 litres/2 pints vegetable stock
4 tbsp lime juice
pinch of cayenne pepper
salt and pepper
2 tbsp snipped chives, to garnish
French bread, to serve

method

1 Put the avocados, garlic, stock, lime juice and cayenne pepper into a food processor or blender and process until the soup is smooth.

2 Season with salt and pepper to taste and leave to chill in the refrigerator until ready to serve. Pour into 4 chilled bowls, garnish with chives and serve with French bread.

hummus with crudités

ingredients

serves 4

175 g/6 oz canned chickpeas
125 ml/4 fl oz tahini
2 garlic cloves
125 ml/4 fl oz lemon juice
2–3 tbsp water
1 tbsp olive oil
1 tbsp chopped fresh parsley
pinch of cayenne pepper
salt

crudités

selection of vegetables,
    including carrots,
    cauliflower and celery

method

1 Drain and rinse the chickpeas. Place them in a blender or food processor with the tahini, garlic and lemon juice and season to taste with salt. Process, gradually adding the water, until smooth and creamy.

2 Scrape the chickpea mixture into a serving bowl and make a hollow in the centre. Pour the olive oil into the hollow and sprinkle with the chopped fresh parsley and the cayenne pepper.

3 Slice the raw vegetables into bite-sized portions and arrange on a large serving platter. Serve with the bowl of hummus.

ham & figs

ingredients

serves 4

350 g / 12 oz or 16 thin slices
   Parma ham
8 ripe fresh figs
pepper

method

1 Using a sharp knife, trim the visible fat from the slices of ham and discard. Arrange the ham on 4 large serving plates, loosely folding it so that it falls into decorative shapes.

2 Cut each fig downwards into quarters from the stalk end, but without cutting all the way through. Gently open out each fruit like a flower and place 2 on each of the 4 large serving plates. Season to taste with pepper and serve at room temperature.

mozzarella & tomatoes

ingredients

serves 4

300 g/10½ oz mozzarella cheese,
    drained and thinly sliced
600 g/1 lb 5 oz tomatoes, sliced
16 fresh basil leaves
125 ml/4 fl oz extra virgin olive oil
salt and pepper

method

1 Arrange the mozzarella cheese and tomato slices on
    4 individual serving plates and season to taste with salt.
    Set aside in a cool place for 30 minutes.

2 Sprinkle the basil leaves over the salad and drizzle
    with the olive oil. Season with pepper and serve the
    salad immediately.

ham & cheese croissant

ingredients

serves 1

1 croissant
1 egg, hard-boiled and sliced
2 thin slices cooked ham, halved
mustard, to taste (optional)
about 25 g/1 oz or 2 slices hard
    cheese, such as Cheddar,
    Gruyère or Emmenthal

method

1 Preheat the grill to medium–high. Slice the croissant horizontally in half, then lay it, cut-sides up, on the rack in the grill pan.

2 Top the croissant with the hard-boiled egg and slices of ham, and spread with a little mustard, if using. Top with the cheese slices, cutting and overlapping them to fit the croissant. Cook under the grill for about 2 minutes, until the cheese has melted. The croissant will be warmed through and beginning to brown around the edges.

3 Invert the top half of the croissant on top of the bottom half. Serve immediately.

spiced scrambled eggs

ingredients

serves 2

4 eggs
150 ml/5 fl oz single cream
pinch of saffron
25 g/1 oz butter
½ tsp ground cumin
½ – 1 tsp harissa paste
1 tsp ground coriander
salt and pepper
2 pieces of freshly toasted bread,
    buttered if wanted, to serve

method

1 Whisk the eggs, cream, salt and pepper and saffron
   together in a bowl.

2 Melt the butter in a saucepan and add the cumin,
   harissa and ground coriander. Cook gently for
   1 minute.

3 Pour in the egg mixture and cook, stirring, for a few
   minutes until the eggs are just set. Serve the spiced
   scrambled eggs on top of the freshly toasted bread.

pear & roquefort open sandwiches

ingredients

serves 2–4

4 slices walnut bread or pain
    Poilâne, about 1 cm/½ inch
    thick
4 thin slices Parma ham
2 ripe pears, such as Conference,
    peeled, halved, cored and
    thinly sliced lengthways
100 g/3½ oz Roquefort cheese,
    very thinly sliced

method

1 Preheat the grill to medium–high. Toast the bread slices
   on the rack in the grill pan until crisp, but not brown,
   on both sides. Do not turn off the grill.

2 Fold or cut the ham slices to cover each slice of bread,
   then divide the pear slices equally between the bread
   slices. Lay the cheese slices on top.

3 Return the slices to the grill until the cheese melts and
   bubbles. Serve immediately.

smoked trout with pears

ingredients

serves 4

55 g/2 oz watercress
1 head radicchio, torn into pieces
4 smoked trout fillets, skinned
2 ripe pears, such as Williams
2 tbsp lemon juice
2 tbsp extra virgin olive oil
3 tbsp soured cream
2 tsp creamed horseradish
salt and pepper
thinly sliced brown bread,
    buttered, to serve

method

1 Place the watercress and radicchio in a bowl. Cut the trout fillets into thin strips and add to the bowl. Cut the pears in half, then thinly slice. Place in a separate bowl, add 4 teaspoons of the lemon juice and toss to coat. Add the pears to the salad.

2 To make the dressing, mix the remaining lemon juice and the olive oil together in a bowl, then season to taste with salt and pepper. Pour the dressing over the salad and toss well. Transfer to a large salad bowl.

3 Mix the sour cream and horseradish together in a separate bowl until thoroughly blended and pour into a small serving bowl. Serve the salad with the horseradish cream and buttered brown bread.

warm goat's cheese salad

ingredients
serves 4

1 small iceberg lettuce,
    torn into pieces
handful of rocket leaves
few radicchio leaves, torn
6 slices French bread
115 g/4 oz goat's cheese, sliced

dressing
4 tbsp extra virgin olive oil
1 tbsp white wine vinegar
salt and pepper

method

1 Divide all the leaves between 4 individual salad bowls.

2 Preheat the grill. Toast one side of the bread under the grill until golden. Place a slice of cheese on top of each untoasted side and toast until the cheese is just melting.

3 Put all the dressing ingredients into a bowl and beat together until combined. Pour over the leaves, tossing to coat.

4 Cut each slice of bread in half and place 3 halves on top of each salad. Toss very gently to combine and serve warm.

tagliatelle with lemon & thyme

ingredients

serves 2–4

350 g/12 oz fresh tagliatelle
85g/3 oz butter
finely grated zest and juice
    of 1 lemon
2 tbsp chopped fresh thyme,
    plus extra sprigs to garnish
salt and pepper

method

1 Cook the pasta in a large saucepan of boiling salted
   water for about 4 minutes, or according to the packet
   instructions, until tender but still firm to the bite.

2 Drain the pasta, keeping about 3 tablespoons of the
   cooking liquid in it. Stir in the butter, grated lemon
   zest and lemon juice, thyme, and salt and pepper, and
   toss well to mix. Serve immediately, garnished with the
   thyme sprigs.

creamy ricotta, mint & garlic pasta

ingredients

serves 4

300 g/10½ oz short fresh
   pasta shapes
140 g/5 oz ricotta cheese
1–2 roasted garlic cloves from
   a jar, finely chopped
150 ml/5 fl oz double cream
1 tbsp chopped fresh mint, plus
   extra sprigs, to garnish
salt and pepper

method

1 Cook the pasta in a large saucepan of boiling salted
   water for about 3 minutes, or according to the packet
   instructions, until tender but still firm to the bite.

2 Beat the ricotta, garlic, cream and chopped mint
   together in a bowl until smooth.

3 Drain the cooked pasta then tip back into the pan.
   Pour in the cheese mixture and toss together.

4 Season with pepper and serve immediately, garnished
   with the sprigs of mint.

microwave herbed fish parcels

ingredients

serves 4

4 firm white fish fillets, such
    as monkfish, about
    115 g/4 oz each
4 tbsp lemon juice
4 tbsp cider or white wine
4 tbsp chopped fresh parsley
4 fresh thyme sprigs
4 fresh rosemary sprigs
4 tomatoes, thinly sliced

method

1 Place the fish fillets in the centre of 4 x 30-cm/12-inch
    squares of baking paper.

2 Sprinkle each fillet with 1 tablespoon of lemon juice
    and 1 tablespoon of cider, followed by 1 tablespoon
    of chopped parsley. Add a sprig of thyme and rosemary
    to each parcel.

3 Arrange the sliced tomatoes over each fillet, overlapping
    them. Fold in the edges of the baking paper squares to
    completely enclose the filling and form parcels. Place
    the parcels in a circle on a heatproof plate, leaving a
    2.5-cm/1-inch space between each parcel, and cook
    in the microwave oven on high for 7 minutes. Serve
    immediately.

peppered tuna steaks

ingredients

serves 4

4 tuna steaks, about 175 g/6 oz
    each
4 tsp sunflower or olive oil
1 tsp salt
2 tbsp mixed pink, green and black
    peppercorns, coarsely crushed

to serve

handful of fresh rocket leaves
lemon wedges
4 baked potatoes (optional)

method

1 Brush the tuna steaks with the oil and sprinkle with salt.

2 Coat the tuna in the crushed peppercorns.

3 Meanwhile, heat a ridged griddle pan or frying pan and, when hot, add the fish and cook over a medium heat for 2–3 minutes on each side. Serve with some rocket leaves and a lemon wedge on the side, and, if using, a baked potato.

strawberry & banana creams

ingredients

serves 4–6

4 large bananas
450 g/1 lb strawberries, hulled,
    plus extra whole strawberries,
    to decorate
300 ml/10 fl oz double cream,
    whipped
granulated or caster sugar,
    if necessary
biscuits, to serve

method

1 Peel the bananas and put in a food processor with the strawberries. Process to a smooth purée and tip the fruit into a large bowl.

2 Gently stir in the whipped cream. Sweeten to taste if needed and spoon into serving glasses.

3 Chill in the refrigerator until you are ready to serve. Decorate with a whole strawberry and serve with light, crunchy biscuits.

french toast with maple syrup

ingredients

serves 4–6

6 eggs
175 ml/6 fl oz milk
¼ tsp ground cinnamon
12 slices day-old plain white bread
about 4 tbsp butter or margarine,
    plus extra to serve
½–1 tbsp sunflower or corn oil
salt
warm maple syrup, to serve

method

1 Preheat the oven to 140°C/275°F/Gas Mark 1.

2 Break the eggs into a large, shallow bowl and beat together with the milk, cinnamon and salt to taste. Add the bread slices and press them down so that they are covered on both sides with the egg mixture. Leave the bread to stand for 1–2 minutes to soak up the egg mixture, turning the slices over once.

3 Melt half the butter with ½ tablespoon of oil in a large frying pan. Add to the pan as many bread slices as will fit in a single layer and cook for 2–3 minutes until golden.

4 Turn the bread slices over and cook until golden brown on the other side. Transfer the French toast to a plate and keep warm in the oven while cooking the remaining bread slices, adding extra oil and butter to the pan, if necessary.

5 Serve the French toast with some butter melting on top and warm maple syrup for pouring over.

grilled cinnamon oranges

ingredients

serves 4

2 large oranges
1 tsp ground cinnamon
1 tbsp demerara sugar

method

1 Cut the oranges in half and discard any pips. Using a sharp knife or a curved grapefruit knife, carefully cut the flesh away from the skin by cutting around the edge of the fruit. Cut across the segments to loosen the flesh into bite-sized pieces that will then spoon out easily.

2 Arrange the orange halves, cut-side up, in a shallow ovenproof dish. Mix the cinnamon with the sugar in a small bowl and sprinkle evenly over the orange halves.

3 Preheat the grill to high. Grill for 3–5 minutes, or until the sugar has caramelized and is golden and bubbling. Serve immediately.

variation

Substitute 2 white grapefruits for the oranges. Drizzle each half with 1 teaspoon of honey and sprinkle with cinnamon, omitting the sugar, before grilling.

meat & poultry

farfalle with gorgonzola & ham

ingredients

serves 4

225 ml/8 fl oz crème fraîche
225 g/8 oz chestnut mushrooms, quartered
400 g/14 oz dried farfalle
85 g/3 oz Gorgonzola cheese, crumbled
1 tbsp chopped fresh flat-leaf parsley, plus extra sprigs to garnish
175 g/6 oz cooked ham, diced
salt and pepper

method

1 Pour the crème fraîche into a saucepan, add the mushrooms and season to taste with salt and pepper. Bring to just below the boil, then lower the heat and simmer very gently, stirring occasionally, until the sauce has thickened.

2 Meanwhile, bring a large pan of lightly salted water to the boil. Add the pasta, bring back to the boil and cook for 8–10 minutes, until tender but still firm to the bite.

3 Remove the pan of mushrooms from the heat and stir in the Gorgonzola cheese until it has melted. Return the pan to a very low heat and stir in the chopped parsley and ham.

4 Drain the pasta and add it to the sauce. Toss lightly, then divide between individual warmed plates, garnish with the sprigs of parsley and serve.

spaghetti carbonara

ingredients

serves 4

450 g/1 lb fresh spaghetti
25 g/1 oz butter
6 rashers streaky bacon, diced
3 eggs
2 tbsp single cream
4 tbsp freshly grated Parmesan
    cheese
salt and pepper
chopped fresh parsley, for
    sprinkling

method

1 Cook the spaghetti in a large saucepan of boiling salted water for about 2–4 minutes, or according to the packet instructions, until tender but still firm to the bite.

2 Meanwhile, heat the butter in a frying pan, add the bacon and cook until crisp. Keep warm.

3 Beat the eggs, cream, cheese, and salt and pepper together in a bowl.

4 As soon as the spaghetti is cooked, drain and return to the pan over a low heat.

5 Add the bacon, and egg and cream mixture, and quickly toss the spaghetti several times until the sauce begins to thicken and the spaghetti is coated. Serve immediately sprinkled with chopped parsley.

florentine ham

ingredients

serves 2

good handful of fresh baby
    spinach leaves
4 slices ham
4 eggs
4 tbsp double cream
55 g/2 oz grated cheese, such
    as Gruyère or Cheddar
salt and pepper

method

1 Put the spinach in a large bowl and pour boiling water
   over it. Leave to stand until the leaves are wilted, then
   drain well on kitchen paper.

2 Line 2 small ovenproof dishes with the ham; it doesn't
   matter if the slices overlap the edges. Spread the
   drained spinach evenly over the top. Season well
   with salt and pepper.

3 Break in the eggs and drizzle over the cream.

4 Preheat the grill to medium–high. Sprinkle with the
   cheese and grill for 8–10 minutes, or until the eggs are
   cooked to your liking and the cheese is bubbling.

sweet & sour pork

ingredients

serves 4

1 tbsp vegetable oil

350 g/12 oz lean pork, cut
    into 5-mm/¼-inch strips

1 large red pepper, deseeded
    and sliced

4 spring onions, trimmed
    and chopped, plus extra
    to garnish

450 g/1 lb canned pineapple
    pieces in juice

2 tbsp cornflour

3 tbsp wine vinegar

juice of 1 lemon

3 tbsp light soy sauce

2 tbsp granulated sugar

salt and pepper

method

1 Heat the oil in a large frying pan, add the pork strips
   and cook for 5 minutes, stirring.

2 Add the red pepper and spring onions to the pan and
   cook for 3 minutes, stirring until they begin to soften.

3 Drain the pineapple juice into a bowl, reserving the
   pineapple pieces, and whisk in the cornflour, vinegar,
   lemon juice, soy sauce, sugar and salt and pepper.

4 Add the mixture to the frying pan and cook over a
   medium heat for 1–2 minutes, stirring until slightly
   thickened. Add the reserved pineapple pieces and
   heat through for 1 minute. Serve immediately,
   garnished with spring onions.

spicy pork meatballs

ingredients

serves 4

675 g/1 lb 8 oz fresh lean
      pork mince
1 garlic clove, finely chopped
1 tsp ground ginger
pinch of ground cloves
½ tsp freshly grated nutmeg
½ tsp ground allspice
½ tsp salt
½ tsp black pepper
2 egg yolks
40 g/1½ oz ground almonds
2–3 tbsp sunflower or olive oil

method

1 Mix the pork mince, garlic, spices, salt, pepper, egg
  yolks and ground almonds together in a large bowl.
  Form into balls and brush with the oil.

2 Preheat the grill. Grill the meatballs, turning from time
  to time for about 8–10 minutes, or until thoroughly
  cooked through.

3 Alternatively, heat the oil in a large frying pan and fry
  the meatballs for about 8–10 minutes, or until cooked
  through. Serve immediately.

ginger pork

ingredients

serves 2

2 tbsp sunflower or olive oil
1-cm/½-inch piece fresh ginger,
    peeled and grated
1 garlic clove, crushed
2 boneless pork steaks,
    cut into thin strips
85 g/3 oz shredded white cabbage
4 tbsp cashew nuts
2 tbsp dark soy sauce
1 tbsp dry white wine
1 tsp granulated sugar
1 tsp sesame oil
salt and pepper

method

1 Heat a wok over a high heat and when smoking,
    add 1 tablespoon of oil, swirling it around the wok.

2 Add the ginger and garlic and cook quickly for
    20 seconds. Add the pork and cook for 3–4 minutes,
    or until just cooked through. Remove the pork, ginger
    and garlic from the wok and keep warm.

3 Add the remaining oil to the wok and when hot, add
    the cabbage and cook for 2–3 minutes until tender.
    Add the cashew nuts and cook for 3 seconds.

4 Return the pork, ginger and garlic to the wok with
    the soy sauce, wine and sugar. Cook for 1 minute
    then add the sesame oil and season to taste with
    salt and pepper. Serve immediately.

orange- & lemon-coated crispy lamb cutlets

ingredients

serves 2

1 garlic clove, crushed

1 tbsp olive oil

2 tbsp finely grated orange zest

2 tbsp finely grated lemon zest

6 lamb cutlets

salt and pepper

orange wedges, to garnish

method

1 Mix the garlic, oil, grated orange zest and lemon zest and seasoning together in a bowl.

2 Preheat the grill to medium–high. Brush the mixture over the lamb cutlets and grill for 4–5 minutes on each side. Serve, garnished with the orange wedges.

beef burgers

ingredients

serves 4

650 g/1 lb 7 oz fresh beef mince
1 red pepper, deseeded and
    finely chopped
1 garlic clove, finely chopped
2 small red chillies, deseeded
    and finely chopped
1 tbsp chopped fresh basil
½ tsp ground cumin
salt and pepper
sprigs of fresh basil, to garnish
hamburger buns, to serve

method

1 Put the minced beef, red pepper, garlic, chillies, chopped basil and cumin into a bowl and mix until well combined. Season with salt and pepper. Using your hands, form the mixture into 4 burger shapes.

2 Preheat the grill to medium–high. Grill the burgers for 5–8 minutes on each side, or until cooked through. Garnish with sprigs of basil and serve in hamburger buns.

teriyaki steak

ingredients

serves 4

4 beef steaks, about 150 g/
   5½ oz each
2 tbsp vegetable oil
200 g/7 oz beansprouts, trimmed
4 spring onions, trimmed
   and finely sliced
salt and pepper

teriyaki sauce

2 tbsp mirin (Japanese rice wine)
2 tbsp sake or pale dry sherry
4 tbsp dark soy sauce
1 tsp granulated or caster sugar

method

1 Season the steaks with salt and pepper and set aside.

2 To make the sauce, combine the mirin, sake, soy sauce and sugar in a bowl, stirring well.

3 Heat 1 tablespoon of oil in a frying pan over a high heat. Add the beansprouts and fry quickly, tossing them in the hot oil for 30 seconds. Remove from the pan and drain on kitchen paper.

4 Add the remaining oil to the pan and when hot add the steaks. Cook for 1–3 minutes on each side, according to how rare you like your meat. Remove from the pan and keep warm.

5 Remove the pan from the heat and add the sauce and spring onions. Return to the heat and simmer for 2 minutes, stirring until the sauce thickens slightly and is glossy.

6 Slice each steak and arrange on a bed of beansprouts. Spoon over the sauce and serve immediately.

stir-fried beef with cashew nuts

ingredients

serves 2

2 tbsp sunflower or olive oil
450 g/1 lb rump steak, cut
    into thin strips
1 tbsp black peppercorns, crushed
2 fresh chillies, deseeded
    and finely chopped
bunch of spring onions, trimmed
    and thinly sliced or chopped
115 g/4 oz cashew nuts

sauce

3 tbsp soy sauce
2 tbsp rice wine or dry sherry
1 tbsp dark brown sugar
1 tsp five spice powder

method

1 Heat the oil in a preheated wok until smoking. Add the steak strips, crushed peppercorns, chillies and spring onions and cook for 3–4 minutes, tossing the wok to cook evenly.

2 Mix all the ingredients for the sauce together in a bowl and pour into the wok. Cook for 3 minutes, tossing the ingredients until everything is heated through.

3 Add the cashew nuts and toss to combine. Serve the stir-fry immediately.

peppered steaks in whisky cream sauce

ingredients

serves 4

3 tbsp black peppercorns, crushed

4 minute steaks, about 175 g/6 oz each

2 tbsp sunflower or olive oil

sprig of parsley and seasonal vegetables, to serve

whisky cream sauce

150 ml/5 fl oz double cream

2 tbsp beef stock

2–3 tbsp malt whisky

method

1 Press the crushed peppercorns firmly into the steaks to coat both sides.

2 Heat the oil in a frying pan and when hot, place the steaks in the pan and cook for 1 minute on each side.

3 Remove the steaks and keep warm. Pour off the oil from the pan.

4 Mix the cream, stock, whisky and any juices from the steaks together in a bowl and pour into the frying pan. Heat through, stirring, then pour over the steaks. Serve immediately with the parsley and seasonal vegetables.

beef & blue cheese wraps

ingredients

serves 4

250 g/9 oz sirloin steak
1 tbsp olive oil
1 tbsp mayonnaise
125 g/4½ oz Stilton cheese,
    crumbled
4 x 25-cm/10-inch wraps
½ small bag watercress
salt and pepper

method

1 Season the steak with salt and pepper.

2 Preheat a non-stick pan until almost smoking. Add the oil, then seal the steak, cooking on both sides for 30 seconds for very rare (or longer according to personal preference). Remove from the pan and set aside for a few minutes. Once the steak has rested, cut into thin strips with a sharp knife.

3 Mix together the mayonnaise and Stilton cheese.

4 Preheat a non-stick pan or griddle pan until almost smoking, then cook the wraps one at a time on both sides for 10 seconds. This will add some colour and also soften the wraps.

5 Divide the steak between the wraps, placing it along the middle of each wrap. Top with the Stilton and mayonnaise mixture, and then with watercress, reserving a little for the garnish. Roll up, cut in half and serve, garnished with the remaining watercress.

chicken satay

ingredients

serves 4

4 tbsp smooth peanut butter
100 ml/3½ fl oz soy sauce
4 skinless, boneless chicken
    breasts, cut into thin strips
freshly cooked rice and lemon
    wedges, to serve

method

1 Mix the peanut butter and soy sauce together in a
   bowl until smooth. Stir in the chicken strips, tossing
   well to coat in the mixture.

2 If you are using wooden skewers, soak them in cold
   water for at least 30 minutes to prevent them from
   burning. Thread the chicken strips onto the skewers.

3 Preheat the grill to high. Grill the skewers for about
   5 minutes on each side until cooked through. Serve
   immediately with rice and lemon wedges.

minced chicken skewers

ingredients

serves 4

450 g/1 lb fresh chicken mince
1 onion, finely chopped
1 fresh red chilli, deseeded
    and chopped
2 tbsp Thai red curry paste
1 tsp palm sugar or soft light
    brown sugar
1 tsp ground coriander
1 tsp ground cumin
1 egg white
8 lemon grass stalks
sprigs of coriander, to garnish
rice with chopped spring onion,
    to serve

method

1 Mix the chicken, onion, chilli, curry paste and sugar together in a bowl to a thick paste. Stir in the ground coriander, cumin and egg white and mix again.

2 Divide the mixture into 8 equal portions and squeeze each one around a lemon grass stalk.

3 Preheat the grill to high. Grill the skewers, turning frequently, for 8 minutes, or until browned and cooked through. Garnish with the coriander sprigs and serve immediately, accompanied by cooked rice with chopped spring onion stirred through it.

fragrant chicken

ingredients

serves 4

1 fresh red chilli, deseeded
    and finely chopped

3 garlic cloves, finely chopped

4 spring onions, trimmed and
    finely chopped

1–2-cm/$^1/_2$–$^1/_4$-inch piece fresh
    ginger, cut into wafer thin slices

1 tsp ground coriander

1 tsp ground cumin

4 tbsp olive oil

4 tbsp pine kernels, lightly
    crushed

4 skinless, boneless chicken
    breasts, cut into thin slices

1 tbsp chopped fresh coriander

salt and pepper

method

1 Combine the chilli, garlic, spring onions, ginger, ground coriander, cumin, 3 tablespoons of oil and the pine kernels in a bowl and season with salt and pepper.

2 Heat the remaining oil in a wok and, when very hot, add the chicken slices. Cook over a high heat for about 4 minutes, or until the chicken is browned all over.

3 Add the chilli mixture and cook for 4–5 minutes, or until the chicken is completely cooked.

4 Stir in the fresh coriander and serve immediately.

chicken with creamy penne

ingredients

serves 2

200 g/7 oz fresh penne pasta
1 tbsp olive oil
2 skinless, boneless chicken breasts
4 tbsp dry white wine
115 g/4 oz frozen peas
5 tbsp double cream
salt
4–5 tbsp chopped fresh parsley,
    to garnish

method

1 Cook the penne in a large saucepan of boiling salted water for about 3–4 minutes, or according to the packet instructions, until tender but still firm to the bite.

2 Meanwhile, heat the oil in a frying pan, add the chicken breasts and cook over a medium heat for about 4 minutes on each side.

3 Pour in the wine and cook over a high heat until it has almost evaporated.

4 Drain the pasta. Add the peas, cream and pasta to the chicken breasts in the frying pan and stir well. Cover and simmer for 2 minutes. Serve immediately garnished with chopped parsley.

duck breasts with citrus glaze

ingredients

serves 4

55 g/2 oz light brown sugar,
    plus extra if needed
finely grated zest and juice
    of 1 orange
finely grated zest and juice
    of 1 large lemon
finely grated zest and juice
    of 1 lime
4 duck breasts, skin on
2 tbsp olive oil
salt and pepper
sugar snap peas and orange
    wedges, to serve

method

1 Put the sugar in a small saucepan, add just enough water to cover and heat gently until dissolved.

2 Add the citrus zests and juices and bring to the boil. Reduce the heat and simmer for about 10 minutes until the zest is soft, and the liquid is syrupy. Remove the pan from the heat. Taste and add a little more sugar if necessary.

3 Meanwhile, score the skin of the duck breasts with a sharp knife in a criss-cross pattern and season with salt and pepper.

4 Heat the oil in a frying pan. Place the duck breasts skin-side up in the pan and cook for 5 minutes on each side until the flesh is just pink. Keep warm.

5 Slice the duck breasts diagonally into 5–6 slices and arrange on warmed plates. Arrange the sugar snap peas and orange wedges on each plate, spoon over the glaze and serve immediately.

honeyed duck stir-fry

ingredients

serves 4

2 tbsp honey
4 tbsp soy sauce
4 skinless duck breasts, sliced
1 tbsp olive oil
bunch of spring onions,
    trimmed and sliced
1 small head Chinese cabbage,
    finely shredded
salt and pepper

method

1 Mix the honey and soy sauce together in a large bowl. Add the duck slices and toss to coat in the mixture.

2 Heat the oil in a wok or frying pan. Add the duck strips (reserve the honey mixture) and cook quickly for 2 minutes until browned.

3 Add the spring onions, Chinese cabbage and the reserved honey mixture. Cook for 3–4 minutes until the duck is cooked but still a little pink in the centre.

4 Season with salt and pepper and serve immediately.

turkey ciabatta with walnuts

ingredients

serves 2

2 ciabatta rolls
100 g/4 oz blue cheese, such as
    Stilton or Danish blue, finely
    diced or crumbled
100 g/4 oz walnuts, chopped
8 large fresh sage leaves,
    finely shredded
4 slices cooked turkey breast
seedless green grapes, to serve

method

1 Preheat the grill to medium–high. Slice the ciabatta rolls in half horizontally and toast the cut sides. Remove the top halves. Turn the bottom halves over and toast the undersides until brown and crisp. When the breads are toasted, set them aside and reduce the heat to a low setting.

2 Meanwhile, mix together the blue cheese, walnuts and sage. Lay 2 turkey slices on the base of each roll and top with the cheese and walnut mixture, piling it up in the middle. Cover with the top of the roll.

3 Warm the rolls under the preheated grill, well away from the heat, for 3–4 minutes, until the bread is hot and the cheese is beginning to melt. Increase the heat slightly, if necessary, to medium but do not turn it up high enough to brown the tops of the rolls before they are warmed through.

4 Serve the hot turkey rolls with some green grapes.

fish & seafood

garlic-sizzled prawns with chilli dipping sauce

ingredients

serves 3–4

2 tbsp sunflower or olive oil

1–2 garlic cloves, crushed

bunch of spring onions, trimmed and chopped

350 g/12 oz raw peeled prawns, with tails left on

chopped fresh chives, to garnish

lime wedges, to serve

chilli dipping sauce

2 tbsp treacle

6 tbsp white wine vinegar

2 tbsp Thai fish sauce or light soy sauce

2 tbsp water

1 garlic clove, crushed

2 tsp grated fresh ginger

2 tsp finely chopped deseeded fresh red chilli

method

1 To make the sauce, heat the treacle, vinegar, fish sauce and water in a small saucepan until boiling. Add the garlic, ginger and chilli and pour into a small serving bowl.

2 Heat the oil in a wok or frying pan and add the garlic and spring onions. Cook over a high heat for 2 minutes then add the prawns, stir-frying them for 2–3 minutes until cooked.

3 Divide between 4 warmed serving plates. Garnish with chives and serve with lime wedges and the chilli dipping sauce.

hot & sour prawn soup

ingredients

serves 2

300 g/10½ oz raw peeled prawns
2 tsp vegetable oil
2 fresh red chillies, sliced
1 garlic clove, sliced
about 750 ml/1⅓ pints fish stock
4 thin slices fresh ginger
2 lemon grass stalks, bruised
5 Thai lime leaves, shredded
2 tsp palm sugar or brown sugar
1 tbsp chilli oil
handful of fresh coriander leaves
dash of lime juice

method

1 Dry fry the prawns in a frying pan or wok until they turn pink. Remove and set aside.

2 Heat the vegetable oil in the same pan, add the chillies and garlic and cook for 30 seconds.

3 Add the stock, ginger, lemon grass, Thai lime leaves and sugar and simmer for 4 minutes. Add the reserved prawns with the chilli oil and coriander and cook for 1–2 minutes.

4 Stir in the lime juice and serve immediately.

prawn toasts

ingredients

serves 2–4

100 g/3½ oz peeled and
  deveined raw prawns
2 egg whites
2 tbsp cornflour
½ tsp sugar
pinch of salt
2 tbsp finely chopped fresh
  coriander leaves
2 slices day-old white bread
vegetable or groundnut oil,
  for deep-frying

method

1 Pound the prawns to a pulp in a mortar with a pestle
  or with the base of a cleaver.

2 Mix the prawns with one of the egg whites and half
  the cornflour in a bowl. Add the sugar and salt, and stir
  in the coriander. Mix the remaining egg white with the
  remaining cornflour in a jug.

3 Remove the crusts from the bread and cut each slice
  into 8 triangles. Brush the top of each piece with the
  egg white and cornflour mixture, then add 1 teaspoon
  of the prawn mixture and spread smoothly over
  the top.

4 Heat enough oil for deep-frying in a wok, deep-fat
  fryer or large, heavy-based saucepan to 180°C/350°F,
  or until a cube of bread browns in 30 seconds. Without
  overcrowding the pan, cook the toasts prawn-side up
  for 2 minutes. Turn and cook for a further 2 minutes
  until beginning to turn golden brown. Remove with
  a slotted spoon, drain on kitchen paper and keep
  warm in a low oven while cooking the remainder
  before serving.

pancetta-wrapped scallops

ingredients

serves 4

16 large fresh scallops
8 slices pancetta, halved
1 tbsp olive oil
juice of 1 lemon
pepper
lemon wedges, to serve

method

1 Wrap each scallop in half a slice of pancetta.

2 Mix the oil, lemon juice and a sprinkling of pepper together in a bowl.

3 Coat the scallops in the mixture and thread onto metal skewers (4 on each skewer). Discard any leftover lemon juice mixture.

4 Preheat the grill to medium–hot. Grill the scallops for 4–5 minutes, turning once until cooked. Serve immediately with lemon wedges.

poached scallops with sweet dill dressing

ingredients

serves 4

12 fresh queen scallops
　　with their corals
finely grated rind and juice
　　of 2 limes
150 ml/5 fl oz dry white wine
bunch of spring onions, trimmed
　　and diagonally sliced
2 tbsp granulated sugar
55 g/2 oz butter
2 tbsp chopped fresh dill
salt and pepper
fresh dill sprigs and lime slices,
　　to garnish

method

1 Put the scallops in a shallow dish. Mix the lime rind, juice, wine, spring onions, salt and pepper, and sugar together in a bowl. Pour the mixture over the scallops and turn them to coat well.

2 Heat the butter in a frying pan. Using a slotted spoon, remove the scallops from the lime mixture and add to the pan, reserving the lime juice mixture. Fry for 2 minutes on each side until almost tender.

3 Stir the lime juice mixture and chopped dill into the pan. Bring to the boil and boil rapidly for 8 minutes until reduced.

4 Serve immediately, garnished with dill sprigs and lime slices.

oysters au gratin

ingredients

serves 2

115 g/4 oz pancetta or streaky
    bacon, diced
25 g/1 oz celery, finely chopped
4 asparagus tips, finely chopped
6 fresh oysters, shucked
25 g/1 oz firm mozzarella cheese,
    grated
salt and pepper

method

1 Cook the pancetta in a small frying pan for 1–2 minutes until crisp. Add the celery and asparagus and season to taste with salt and pepper.

2 Spoon the pancetta and asparagus mixture over the oysters. Sprinkle over the grated cheese.

3 Preheat the grill to medium–high. Grill the oysters for 3–4 minutes, or until the cheese is golden brown and melted. Serve immediately.

wine-steamed mussels

ingredients

serves 4

115 g/4 oz butter
1 shallot, chopped
3 garlic cloves, finely chopped
2 kg/4 lb 8 oz live mussels,
    scrubbed and beards removed
225 ml/8 fl oz dry white wine
½ tsp salt
4 tbsp chopped fresh parsley
pepper

method

1 Melt half the butter in a very large saucepan over a low heat. Add the shallot and garlic and cook for 2 minutes. Add the mussels, discarding any with broken shells or any that refuse to close when tapped, wine, salt and a sprinkling of pepper.

2 Cover, bring to the boil, then boil for 3 minutes, shaking the pan from time to time.

3 Remove the mussels from the pan with a slotted spoon and place in individual serving bowls. Discard any mussels that remain closed.

4 Mix the remaining butter with the parsley in a small bowl and stir the mixture into the cooking juices in the pan. Bring to the boil and pour over the mussels. Serve immediately.

crab & fennel wraps

ingredients

serves 4

250 g/9 oz baby fennel
150 g/5½ oz fresh or canned
    white crabmeat
4 tbsp mayonnaise
grated rind and juice of 1 lemon
small bunch of fresh flat-leaf
    parsley, shredded
4 x 25-cm/10-inch Mediterranean
    herb wraps
salt and pepper

method

1 Cut the fennel in half lengthways and then slice thinly.

2 Place the sliced fennel in a bowl with the crabmeat, mayonnaise, lemon rind and juice and parsley and salt and pepper. Mix well.

3 Leave for 5 minutes to allow the lemon juice to wilt the fennel slightly.

4 Preheat a non-stick pan or griddle pan until almost smoking, then cook the wraps one at a time on each side for 10 seconds. This will add some colour and also soften the wraps.

5 Give the filling mixture another stir and then divide between the wraps, placing one portion in the middle of each wrap. Fold in the ends, roll up, cut in half at an angle and serve.

crab fritters with avocado salsa

ingredients

serves 4

200 g/7 oz lightly cooked
   sweetcorn kernels
70 g/2½ oz plain flour
2 eggs, beaten
300 g/10½ oz fresh or canned
   white crabmeat
1 small bunch fresh parsley,
   chopped
3–4 tbsp olive oil
salt and pepper
lime wedges, to serve

avocado salsa

1 small red onion, finely chopped
1 red pepper, deseeded and diced
1 yellow pepper, deseeded and
   diced
1 avocado, stoned and diced
1 mango, stoned and diced
4 tomatoes, diced
finely grated rind and juice
   of 2 limes
1 large bunch fresh coriander,
   chopped
salt and pepper

method

1 First make the salsa. Put the onion in a bowl. Add the peppers. Add the avocado and mango to the bowl, then add the tomatoes. Stir in the lime rind and juice and coriander. Season to taste with salt and pepper.

2 Put the sweetcorn kernels, flour and eggs in a separate bowl and stir until well mixed. Lightly fold in the crabmeat and parsley, and season to taste with salt and pepper.

3 Heat the oil in a large frying pan over a medium–high heat. Drop spoonfuls of the batter into the hot oil and cook in batches for 2–3 minutes on each side until crisp and golden. Remove and drain on kitchen paper. Serve immediately with the salsa and the lime wedges.

salmon with lemon & olive dressing

ingredients

serves 4

2 tbsp olive oil
4 salmon fillets, skin on,
    about 175 g/6 oz each
juice of ½ lemon
salt
freshly boiled new potatoes
    and green salad, to serve

dressing

1 handful fresh basil leaves
2 tbsp snipped fresh chives
1 garlic clove, crushed
1 tsp wholegrain mustard
½ tsp caster sugar
juice of ½ lemon
200 ml/7 fl oz extra virgin
    olive oil
rind of ½ preserved lemon,
    finely chopped
10 stoned black olives,
    finely chopped

method

1 Preheat the oven to 200°C/400°F/Gas Mark 6.

2 To make the dressing, put the herbs, garlic, mustard, sugar, lemon juice and extra virgin olive oil in a blender or food processor and blend until smooth. Pour the mixture into a small saucepan, add the preserved lemon rind and olives and warm over a gentle heat.

3 Meanwhile, heat the olive oil in a frying pan over a medium heat, add the salmon fillets, skin-side down, and cook for 3 minutes, or until the skin is golden and crisp. Lay the fish in a roasting tin, skin-side up, squeeze over the lemon juice and season with a little salt.

4 Roast in the preheated oven for 5 minutes, or until the fish is just cooked through – the exact timing will depend on the thickness of the fillets. Serve immediately, with the dressing spooned over the fish, accompanied by new potatoes and a green salad.

smoked salmon pâté

ingredients

serves 4–6

450 g/1 lb smoked salmon,
    chopped into small pieces
1 tsp chopped fresh thyme
finely grated rind and juice
    of 1 small lemon
2 tbsp soft unsalted butter
85 g/3 oz soft cream cheese
pinch of paprika
pinch of cayenne pepper
pepper
crispbreads, to serve

method

1 Put the smoked salmon, thyme, lemon rind and juice
  in a food processor or blender and process until just
  combined together.

2 Scrape down the sides of the bowl and add the butter
  and cheese. Season lightly with the paprika, cayenne
  pepper and black pepper.

3 Process again until the mixture is blended, but not
  completely smooth – it should still have a slightly
  rough texture. Taste the pâté, and adjust the seasoning
  if necessary.

4 Transfer to an airtight container. Cover with clingfilm
  and leave to chill in the refrigerator until firm. Remove
  from the refrigerator at least 15 minutes before eating
  and serve with crispbreads.

smoked salmon tagliatelle

ingredients

serves 4

350 g/12 oz dried tagliatelle
2 tbsp olive oil
1 garlic clove, finely chopped
115 g/4 oz smoked salmon,
    cut into thin strips
55 g/2 oz rocket
salt and pepper

method

1 Bring a large, heavy-based saucepan of lightly salted water to the boil. Add the pasta, return to the boil and cook for 8–10 minutes, or until tender but still firm to the bite.

2 Just before the end of the cooking time, heat the olive oil in a heavy-based frying pan. Add the garlic and cook over a low heat, stirring constantly, for 1 minute. Do not allow the garlic to brown or it will taste bitter.

3 Add the salmon and rocket. Season to taste with pepper and cook, stirring constantly, for 1 minute. Remove the frying pan from the heat.

4 Drain the pasta and transfer to a warmed serving dish. Add the smoked salmon and rocket mixture, toss lightly and serve.

variation

For a creamier version of this pasta dish, add 250 g/9 oz plain yogurt, mixed with a squeeze of lemon juice. Replace the rocket with a handful of chopped fresh dill, if preferred.

teriyaki salmon fillets with chinese noodles

ingredients

serves 4

4 salmon fillets, about
    200 g/7 oz each
125 ml/4 fl oz teriyaki marinade
1 shallot, sliced
2-cm/¾-inch piece fresh ginger,
    finely chopped
2 carrots, sliced
115 g/4 oz closed-cup
    mushrooms, sliced
1.2 litres/2 pints vegetable stock
250 g/9 oz dried medium egg
    noodles
115 g/4 oz frozen peas
175 g/6 oz Chinese cabbage,
    shredded
4 spring onions, sliced

method

1 Arrange the salmon fillets, skin side up, in a dish just
large enough to fit them in a single layer. Mix the
teriyaki marinade with the shallot and ginger in a small
bowl and pour over the salmon. Cover with clingfilm
and leave to marinate in the refrigerator for at least
1 hour, turning halfway through the marinating time.

2 Put the carrots, mushrooms and stock into a large
saucepan. Arrange the salmon, skin side down, on a
shallow baking tray. Pour the fish marinade into the
pan of vegetables and stock and bring to the boil.
Reduce the heat, cover and simmer for 10 minutes.

3 Meanwhile, preheat the grill to medium. Grill the
salmon for 10–15 minutes, until the flesh flakes easily.
Remove from under the grill and keep warm.

4 Add the noodles and peas to the stock and return
to the boil. Reduce the heat, cover and simmer for
5 minutes, or until the noodles are tender. Stir in the
Chinese leaves and spring onions and heat through for
1 minute. Divide the noodles and vegetables between
4 warmed serving bowls and top each with a salmon
fillet. Serve immediately.

swordfish steaks with lemon dressing

ingredients

serves 4

5 tbsp olive oil, plus extra for
    brushing
juice of ½ large or 1 small lemon
2 garlic cloves, well crushed
2 tsp finely chopped fresh oregano
2 tbsp chopped fresh parsley
4 swordfish steaks, about
    175 g/6 oz each
salt and pepper
lemon wedges, to garnish
freshly cooked asparagus,
    to serve

method

1 Put the oil, lemon juice, garlic and herbs with a little salt and pepper to taste, in a screw-top jar and shake well to combine.

2 Preheat a ridged griddle pan over a high heat. Pat the swordfish steaks dry with kitchen paper and lightly brush with oil on both sides. When the griddle pan is very hot, add the swordfish steaks and cook for 2 minutes on each side, or until cooked through but still moist inside.

3 Serve immediately, accompanied by freshly cooked asparagus and garnished with lemon wedges. Shake the lemon dressing again and drizzle it over the fish.

lemon & parsley crusted monkfish

ingredients

serves 4

4 tbsp sunflower oil
   or melted butter
4 tbsp fresh breadcrumbs
4 tbsp chopped fresh parsley
finely grated rind of 1 large lemon
4 monkfish fillets, 140–175 g/
   5–6 oz each
salt and pepper
fresh sprigs of parsley,
   to garnish
4 potatoes, peeled, cubed
   and deep-fried, to serve
   (optional)

method

1 Preheat the oven to 180°C/350°F/Gas Mark 4.

2 Mix the oil, breadcrumbs, parsley and lemon rind with a
   sprinkling of salt and pepper together in a bowl to give
   a smooth mixture.

3 Place the fish fillets on a large roasting tray. Divide the
   breadcrumb mixture between them and press it down
   carefully onto the fish with your fingers to ensure it
   covers the fillets.

4 Bake in the oven for 7–8 minutes or until the fish is
   cooked. Garnish with fresh sprigs of parsley, and serve
   with deep-fried potato cubes, if using.

fish goujons with chilli mayonnaise

ingredients

serves 4

200 g/7 oz plain flour
3 eggs
140 g/5 oz matzo meal
450 g/1 lb firm white fish,
    such as monkfish,
    cut into strips
sunflower or groundnut oil,
    for frying
salt and pepper

chilli mayonnaise

2 tbsp sweet chilli sauce
4–5 tbsp mayonnaise

method

1 Mix the flour with plenty of salt and pepper on a large flat plate. Beat the eggs in a bowl and spread the matzo meal out on another flat plate.

2 Dip the fish pieces into the seasoned flour, then into the beaten egg, then into the matzo meal, ensuring a generous coating.

3 Pour the oil into a non-stick or heavy-based frying pan to give a depth of 1 cm/½ inch, then heat it up. Cook the fish pieces in batches for a few minutes, turning once, until golden and cooked through.

4 To make the chilli mayonnaise, beat the chilli sauce and mayonnaise together in a bowl until combined.

5 Transfer the fish to warmed plates or glasses and serve with the chilli mayonnaise on the side.

seafood kebabs

ingredients

serves 2–4

450 g/1 lb skinless, boneless fish,
  such as monkfish, swordfish
  and halibut
1 lemon, cut into 8 wedges
8 bay leaves
3 tbsp olive oil

method

1 If you are using wooden skewers, soak them in cold
  water for at least 30 minutes before using to prevent
  them from burning.

2 Cut the fish into cubes and thread onto the skewers
  alternately with the lemon and bay leaves.

3 Preheat the grill to medium–hot. Brush the kebabs
  with oil and grill for about 4 minutes on each side until
  the fish is cooked. Serve immediately.

spicy tuna fish cakes

ingredients

serves 4

4 tbsp plain flour
200 g/7 oz canned tuna in oil,
    drained
2–3 tbsp curry paste
1 spring onion, trimmed and
    finely chopped
1 egg, beaten
sunflower or groundnut oil,
    for frying
salt and pepper
rocket leaves, to serve

method

1 Mix the flour with plenty of salt and pepper on a large flat plate.

2 Mash the tuna with the curry paste, spring onion and beaten egg in a large bowl. Form into 4 fish cakes and dust in the seasoned flour.

3 Heat the oil in a frying pan, add the fish cakes and fry for 3–4 minutes on each side until crisp and golden. Serve on a bed of rocket leaves.

lentil & tuna salad

ingredients

serves 4

1 small red onion, finely chopped
2 ripe tomatoes, deseeded and
    finely diced
400 g/14 oz canned lentils, drained
185 g/6½ oz canned tuna, drained
2 tbsp chopped fresh coriander
pepper

dressing

3 tbsp virgin olive oil
1 tbsp lemon juice
1 tsp wholegrain mustard
1 garlic clove, crushed
½ tsp ground cumin
½ tsp ground coriander

method

1 To make the dressing, whisk together the virgin olive oil, lemon juice, mustard, garlic, cumin and ground coriander in a small bowl until thoroughly combined. Set aside until required.

2 Mix together the chopped onion, chopped tomatoes and drained lentils in a large bowl.

3 Flake the tuna with a fork and stir it into the onion, tomato and lentil mixture. Stir in the chopped fresh coriander and mix well.

4 Pour the dressing over the lentil and tuna salad and season with pepper to taste. Serve immediately.

vegetarian

provençal frittata

ingredients

serves 2–4

3 tbsp sunflower or olive oil
1 garlic clove, chopped
225 g/8 oz fresh or frozen spinach
handful of cherry tomatoes,
    halved
6 eggs, whisked
salt and pepper
cherry tomatoes on the vine,
    to serve (optional)

method

1 Heat the oil in a large frying pan, add the garlic and cook for 1 minute then add the spinach and cook for a further 1 minute until wilted.

2 Season with salt and pepper, add the halved cherry tomatoes to the pan and cook for 1 minute.

3 Pour the eggs into the frying pan, stirring, and cook for 4–5 minutes until set. Serve hot or cold cut into wedges, with cherry tomatoes on the vine, if using.

mixed herb omelette

ingredients

serves 1

2 large eggs
2 tbsp milk
40 g/1½ oz butter
leaves from 1 fresh flat-leaf
    parsley sprig
1 fresh chervil sprig
2 freshly snipped chives
salt and pepper
fresh salad leaves, to serve

method

1 Break the eggs into a bowl. Add the milk and salt and pepper to taste, and quickly beat until just blended.

2 Heat a 20-cm/8-inch omelette pan or frying pan over a medium–high heat until very hot and you can feel the heat rising from the surface. Add 25 g/1 oz of the butter and use a spatula to rub it over the base and around the side of the pan as it melts.

3 As soon as the butter stops sizzling, pour in the eggs. Shake the pan forwards and backwards over the heat and use the spatula to stir the eggs around the pan in a circular motion. Do not scrape the base of the pan.

4 As the omelette begins to set, use the spatula to push the cooked egg from the edge towards the centre, so that the remaining uncooked egg comes in contact with the hot base of the pan. Continue doing this for 3 minutes, or until the omelette looks set on the bottom but is still slightly runny on top.

5 Put the herbs in the centre of the omelette. Tilt the pan away from the handle, so that the omelette slides towards the edge of the pan. Use the spatula to fold the top half of the omelette over the herbs. Slide the omelette onto a plate, then rub the remaining butter over the top. Serve immediately, accompanied by fresh salad leaves.

caramel-topped brie

ingredients

serves 4

2 tbsp water
175 g/6 oz granulated sugar
1 whole mini Brie cheese
8 oatcakes and 4 handfuls fresh,
    washed white grapes,
    to serve (optional)

method

1 Heat the water and sugar in a saucepan over a low heat until the sugar has dissolved completely.

2 Increase the heat and cook steadily until the sugar is a dark golden colour.

3 Remove the pan from the heat then immediately pour over the Brie on a plate and leave to set. Serve at room temperature: crack the caramel before serving, with oatcakes and fresh grapes, if using.

goat's cheese tarts

ingredients
makes 12

butter, for greasing
400 g/14 oz packet ready-rolled
    puff pastry
plain flour, for dusting
1 egg, beaten
3 tbsp onion or tomato relish
3 x 115-g/4-oz goat's cheese
    logs, sliced
olive oil, for drizzling
pepper

method

1 Preheat the oven to 200°C/400°F/Gas Mark 6 and grease several baking trays.

2 Lay the pastry on a lightly floured work surface and cut out as many 7.5-cm/3-inch rounds as possible.

3 Place the rounds on the baking trays and press gently about 2.5 cm/1 inch from the edge of each with a smaller 5-cm/2-inch pastry cutter.

4 Brush the rounds with beaten egg and prick with a fork.

5 Top each circle with a little relish and a slice of goat's cheese. Drizzle with oil and sprinkle over a little pepper.

6 Bake for 8–10 minutes, or until the pastry is crisp and the cheese is bubbling. Serve warm.

vegetable tartlets

ingredients

makes 12

butter, for greasing
12 ready-baked puff pastry cases
2 tbsp olive oil
1 red pepper, deseeded and diced
1 garlic clove, crushed
1 small onion, finely chopped
225 g/8 oz ripe tomatoes, chopped
1 tbsp torn fresh basil
1 tsp fresh or dried thyme
salt and pepper
green salad, to serve

method

1 Preheat the oven to 200°C/400°F/Gas Mark 6 and grease several baking trays.

2 Place the ready-baked pastry cases on the prepared baking trays.

3 Heat the oil in a frying pan, add the pepper, garlic and onion and cook over a high heat for about 3 minutes until soft.

4 Add the tomatoes, herbs and seasoning and spoon into the pastry cases.

5 Bake in the preheated oven for about 5 minutes, or until the filling is piping hot. Serve warm with a green salad.

pizza express

ingredients

serves 4-6

1 ciabatta loaf, sliced horizontally
   or 23-cm/9-inch thin-crust
   pizza base
fresh basil leaves, torn

tomato topping

150 ml/5 fl oz tomato passata
3 tbsp tomato purée
2 garlic cloves, crushed
pinch of sugar
handful of cherry tomatoes
salt and pepper

method

1 Preheat the oven to 200°C/400°F/Gas Mark 6.

2 To make the tomato topping, mix the passata, tomato purée, garlic, sugar and salt and pepper together in a bowl. Spread over the ready-made pizza base and scatter with the cherry tomatoes.

3 Bake in the oven for 8–10 minutes until hot and bubbling. Scatter the pizza with fresh basil leaves and serve immediately.

variation

Before baking, top the tomato mixture with 115 g/4 oz drained roasted peppers from a jar and a few black olives. Scatter over 250 g/9 oz grated mozzarella and a handful of grated or shaved Parmesan cheese over the top then bake in the oven.

garlic & broccoli crostini

ingredients

serves 6

500 g/1 lb 2 oz broccoli, stems trimmed and cut into lengths short enough to fit on the crostini
100 ml/3½ fl oz olive oil
1 small bunch wild garlic, rinsed, patted dry and chopped
1–2 red chillies, deseeded and finely chopped
6 slices good-quality country-style bread
salt and pepper

method

1 Preheat the oven to 190°C/375°F/Gas Mark 5.

2 Cook the broccoli in a large saucepan of salted water for 10 minutes, or until just tender. Drain well and set aside.

3 Heat about one third of the oil in a wok or large frying pan over a high heat, add the wild garlic and chilli and stir-fry for 2 minutes. Add the broccoli, season to taste with salt and pepper and stir-fry for 3–4 minutes until hot and crisp.

4 Meanwhile, drizzle the remaining oil evenly over the bread slices and bake in the preheated oven for 10 minutes, or until crisp and golden.

5 Divide the broccoli mixture between the crostini, add a grinding of pepper, and serve immediately.

quesadillas

ingredients

serves 4

4 tbsp finely chopped fresh
    jalapeño chillies
1 onion, chopped
1 tbsp red wine vinegar
5 tbsp extra virgin olive oil
300–400 g/10½–14 oz
    canned sweetcorn
8 soft flour tortillas

method

1 Put the chillies, onion, vinegar and 4 tablespoons of
    olive oil in a food processor or blender and process
    until finely chopped.

2 Tip into a bowl and stir in the sweetcorn.

3 Heat the remaining oil in a frying pan, add a tortilla
    and cook for 1 minute until golden.

4 Spread one eighth of the chilli mixture over the tortilla
    and fold over.

5 Cook for 2–3 minutes until golden and the filling is
    heated through. Remove the quesadillas from the pan
    and keep warm. Repeat with the other tortillas and
    filling. Serve immediately.

falafel burgers

ingredients

serves 4

800 g/1 lb 12 oz canned chickpeas,
  drained and rinsed
1 small onion, chopped
rind and juice of 1 lime
2 tsp ground coriander
2 tsp ground cumin
6 tbsp plain flour
4 tbsp olive oil
4 sprigs fresh basil, to garnish
ready-made tomato salsa, to serve

method

1 Put the chickpeas, onion, lime rind and juice and
  the spices into a food processor and process to
  a coarse paste.

2 Tip the mixture out onto a clean work surface
  or chopping board and shape into 4 burgers.

3 Spread the flour out on a large flat plate and use
  to coat the burgers.

4 Heat the oil in a large frying pan, add the burgers and
  cook for 2 minutes on each side until crisp. Garnish
  with basil and serve with tomato salsa.

crispy spring rolls

ingredients

serves 4

2 tbsp vegetable or groundnut
    oil, plus extra for deep-frying
6 spring onions, cut into
    5-cm/2-inch lengths
1 fresh green chilli, deseeded
    and chopped
1 carrot, cut into thin batons
1 courgette, cut into thin batons
1/2 red pepper, deseeded
    and thinly sliced
115 g/4 oz beansprouts,
    drained and rinsed
    if canned
115 g/4 oz canned bamboo
    shoots, drained and rinsed
3 tbsp Thai soy sauce
1–2 tbsp chilli sauce
8 spring roll wrappers

method

1 Heat the oil in a preheated wok or large frying pan
   over a high heat. Add the spring onions and chilli and
   stir-fry for 30 seconds. Add the carrot, courgette and
   red pepper and stir-fry for 1 minute. Remove from the
   heat and stir in the beansprouts, bamboo shoots, soy
   sauce and chilli sauce. Taste and add more soy sauce
   or chilli sauce if necessary.

2 Lay a spring roll wrapper on a work surface and spoon
   some of the vegetable mixture diagonally across the
   centre. Roll one corner over the filling and flip the sides
   of the wrapper over the top, to enclose the filling.
   Continue to roll up to make an enclosed parcel.
   Repeat with the remaining wrappers and filling to
   make 8 spring rolls.

3 Heat the oil for deep-frying in a preheated wok or
   large frying pan to 180°C/350°F, or until a cube of
   bread browns in 30 seconds. Add the spring rolls, in
   2 batches, and cook until crisp and golden brown.
   Remove with a slotted spoon, drain on kitchen paper
   and keep the first batch hot while you cook the
   remaining spring rolls, then serve immediately.

filo-wrapped asparagus

ingredients

serves 4

20 asparagus spears
5 sheets filo pastry
lemon wedges, to serve

cheese dip

85 g/3 oz natural cottage cheese
1 tbsp semi-skimmed milk
4 spring onions, trimmed and
    finely chopped
2 tbsp chopped fresh mixed
    herbs, such as basil, mint
    and tarragon
pepper

method

1 To make the dip, put the cottage cheese in a bowl and add the milk. Beat until smooth, then stir in the spring onions, chopped herbs and pepper to taste. Place in a serving bowl, cover lightly with clingfilm and chill in the refrigerator until required.

2 Cut off and discard the woody ends of the asparagus and shave with a vegetable peeler to remove any woody parts from the spears.

3 Preheat the oven to 190°C/375°F/Gas Mark 5.

4 Cut the filo pastry into quarters and place one sheet on a work surface. Brush lightly with water then place a spear at one end. Roll up to encase the spear, and place on a large baking tray. Repeat until all the asparagus spears are wrapped in pastry.

5 Bake in the preheated oven for 10–12 minutes, or until the pastry is golden. Serve the spears with lemon wedges and the dip on the side.

asparagus with lemon butter sauce

ingredients

serves 4

800 g/1 lb 12 oz asparagus
    spears, trimmed
1 tbsp olive oil
salt and pepper

lemon butter sauce
juice of ½ lemon
2 tbsp water
100 g/3½ oz butter,
    cut into cubes
pepper

method

1 Preheat the oven to 200°C/400°F/Gas Mark 6.

2 Lay the asparagus spears out in a single layer on a large baking sheet. Drizzle over the oil, season to taste with salt and pepper and roast in the preheated oven for 10 minutes, or until just tender.

3 Meanwhile, make the sauce. Pour the lemon juice into a saucepan and add the water. Heat for a minute or so, then slowly add the butter, cube by cube, stirring constantly until it has all been incorporated. Season to taste with pepper and serve immediately, drizzled over the asparagus.

chinese-style gingered vegetables

ingredients

serves 2

1 tbsp sunflower or groundnut oil

2.5-cm/1-inch piece fresh ginger, peeled and grated

1 onion, thinly sliced

115 g/4 oz frozen French beans, cut into small pieces

450 g/1 lb bag frozen mixed vegetables

150 ml/5 fl oz water

2 heaped tbsp dark brown sugar

2 tbsp cornflour

4 tbsp malt vinegar

4 tbsp soy sauce

1 tsp ground ginger

method

1 Heat the oil in a wok or large frying pan, add the grated ginger and fry for 1 minute. Remove from the wok or pan and drain on kitchen paper.

2 Reduce the heat slightly and add the vegetables and water to the wok.

3 Cover with a lid or foil and cook for 5–6 minutes, or until the vegetables are tender.

4 Mix the sugar, cornflour, malt vinegar, soy sauce and ground ginger together in a bowl. Increase the heat to medium and add the mixture to the vegetables in the wok. Simmer for 1 minute, stirring, until thickened.

5 Return the ginger to the wok and stir to mix well. Heat through for 2 minutes and then serve immediately.

tofu stir-fry

ingredients

serves 4

2 tbsp sunflower or olive oil
350 g/12 oz firm tofu, cubed
225 g/8 oz pak choi,
    roughly chopped
1 garlic clove, chopped
4 tbsp sweet chilli sauce
2 tbsp light soy sauce

method

1 Heat 1 tablespoon of oil in a wok, add the tofu in batches and stir-fry for 2–3 minutes until golden. Remove and set aside.

2 Add the pak choi to the wok and stir-fry for a few seconds until tender and wilted. Remove and set aside.

3 Add the remaining oil to the wok, then add the garlic and stir-fry for 30 seconds.

4 Stir in the chilli sauce and soy sauce and bring to the boil.

5 Return the tofu and pak choi to the wok and toss gently until coated in the sauce. Serve immediately.

variation

Additional vegetables that you can include in the stir-fry include spring onions, beansprouts, cherry tomatoes and peppers.

wilted spinach, yogurt & walnut salad

ingredients

serves 2

450 g/1 lb fresh spinach leaves
1 onion, chopped
1 tbsp olive oil
225 ml/8 fl oz natural yogurt
1 garlic clove, finely chopped
2 tbsp chopped toasted walnuts
2–3 tsp chopped fresh mint
salt and pepper
pitta bread, to serve

method

1 Put the spinach and onion into a saucepan, cover and cook gently for a few minutes until the spinach has just wilted.

2 Add the oil and cook for a further 5 minutes. Season to taste with salt and pepper.

3 Combine the yogurt and garlic in a bowl.

4 Put the spinach and onion into a serving bowl and pour over the yogurt mixture. Scatter over the walnuts and chopped mint and serve with pitta bread.

hot tomato & basil salad

ingredients

serves 6

700 g/1 lb 9 oz cherry tomatoes
1 garlic clove, crushed
2 tbsp capers, drained and rinsed
1 tsp granulated sugar
4 tbsp olive oil
2 tbsp torn fresh basil

method

1 Preheat the oven to 200°C/400°F/Gas Mark 6.

2 Stir the tomatoes, garlic, capers and sugar together in a bowl and tip into a roasting tin.

3 Pour over the oil and toss to coat.

4 Cook in the oven for 10 minutes until the tomatoes are hot.

5 Remove from the oven and tip into a heatproof serving bowl. Scatter over the basil and serve immediately.

moroccan carrot & orange salad

ingredients

serves 4

450 g/1 lb carrots, peeled
1 tbsp olive oil
2 tbsp lemon juice
pinch of granulated sugar
2 large oranges, peeled and cut
    into segments (any juices
    reserved)
55 g/2 oz raisins
1 tsp ground cinnamon
2 tbsp toasted pine kernels

method

1 Grate the carrots into a large bowl.

2 In a separate bowl, combine the oil, lemon juice, sugar and any orange juice reserved from the preparing of the orange segments.

3 Toss the orange segments with the carrots and stir in the raisins and cinnamon.

4 Pour over the dressing and scatter over the pine kernels just before serving.

avocado salad with lime dressing

ingredients

serves 4

60 g/2¼oz mixed red and green
    lettuce leaves
60 g/2¼oz wild rocket
4 spring onions, finely diced
5 tomatoes, sliced
25 g/1 oz shelled walnuts,
    toasted and chopped
2 avocados
1 tbsp lemon juice

lime dressing

1 tbsp lime juice
1 tsp French mustard
1 tbsp crème fraîche
1 tbsp chopped fresh parsley
    or coriander
3 tbsp extra virgin olive oil
pinch of sugar
salt and pepper

method

1 Wash and drain the lettuce and rocket if necessary.
    Shred all the salad leaves and arrange in the bottom
    of a large salad bowl. Add the spring onions, tomatoes
    and walnuts.

2 Cut the avocados in half lengthways, then remove and
    discard the stones. Cut the flesh into thin slices or small
    chunks, then brush with the lemon juice to prevent
    discoloration. Transfer to the salad bowl and mix
    together gently.

3 Place all the dressing ingredients, with salt and pepper
    to taste, in a screw-top jar, screw on the lid tightly and
    shake well until thoroughly combined. Drizzle the
    dressing over the salad and serve immediately.

greek salad

ingredients
serves 4

4 tomatoes, cut into wedges
1 onion, sliced
½ cucumber, cut into pieces
225 g/8 oz kalamata olives, stoned
225 g/8 oz feta cheese
    (drained weight), cubed
2 tbsp fresh coriander leaves
fresh flat-leaf parsley sprigs,
    to garnish
pitta bread, to serve

dressing

5 tbsp extra virgin olive oil
2 tbsp white wine vinegar
1 tbsp lemon juice
½ tsp sugar
1 tbsp chopped fresh coriander
salt and pepper

method

1 To make the dressing, place all the dressing ingredients, with salt and pepper to taste, in a large bowl and mix together well.

2 Add the tomatoes, onion, cucumber, olives, cheese and coriander to the bowl. Toss all the ingredients together, then divide between individual serving bowls. Garnish with parsley sprigs and serve with pitta bread.

raspberry & feta salad with couscous

ingredients

serves 6

350 g/12 oz couscous
600 ml/1 pint boiling
vegetable stock
350 g/12 oz fresh raspberries
small bunch of fresh basil
225 g/8 oz feta cheese (drained
weight), cubed or crumbled
2 courgettes, thinly sliced
4 spring onions, trimmed and
diagonally sliced
55 g/2 oz pine kernels, toasted
grated rind of 1 lemon

dressing

1 tbsp white wine vinegar
1 tbsp balsamic vinegar
4 tbsp extra virgin olive oil
juice of 1 lemon
salt and pepper

method

1 Put the couscous in a large, heatproof bowl and pour over the stock. Stir well, cover and leave to soak until all the stock has been absorbed.

2 Pick over the raspberries, discarding any that are overripe. Shred the basil leaves.

3 Transfer the couscous to a large serving bowl and stir well to break up any lumps. Add the cheese, courgettes, spring onions, raspberries and pine kernels. Stir in the basil and lemon rind and gently toss all the ingredients together.

4 Put all the dressing ingredients in a screw-top jar, screw on the lid and shake until well blended. Pour over the salad and serve immediately.

grilled halloumi with herbed couscous

ingredients

serves 4

450 g/1 lb halloumi cheese,
    cut into 5-mm/¼-inch slices
4 tbsp chilli oil

herbed couscous
400 ml/14 fl oz hot
    vegetable stock
225 g/8 oz couscous
2 tbsp chopped fresh mixed herbs
2 tsp lemon juice
1 tbsp olive oil

method

1 Put the cheese slices in a bowl, pour over the chilli oil
   and toss well to coat the cheese.

2 Preheat the grill to high and line the grill rack with foil.
   Place the cheese on the grill rack and grill for 2–3
   minutes on each side until golden.

3 Meanwhile, stir the hot stock into the couscous in a
   large bowl. Cover and leave to stand for 5 minutes.

4 Stir the herbs, lemon juice and olive oil into the
   couscous. Serve with the grilled halloumi cheese.

pasta with chicory & walnuts

ingredients

serves 4

3 tbsp olive oil
2 garlic cloves, crushed
3 heads chicory, sliced
1 tbsp runny honey
100 g/3½ oz walnuts
450 g/1 lb dried penne pasta
salt and pepper

method

1 Heat the oil in a frying pan over a low heat, add the garlic and chicory and cook, stirring, for 3–4 minutes until the chicory begins to wilt. Stir in the honey and walnuts and cook, stirring occasionally, for a further 4–5 minutes. Season to taste with salt and pepper.

2 Meanwhile, cook the pasta in a large saucepan of lightly salted boiling water according to the packet instructions, or until tender but still firm to the bite. Drain and toss with the chicory mixture. Serve immediately.

pasta with spicy olive sauce

ingredients

serves 2–4

350 g/12 oz fresh pasta shapes

½ tsp salt, plus extra for cooking
the pasta

6 tbsp olive oil

½ tsp freshly grated nutmeg

½ tsp pepper

1 garlic clove, crushed

2 tbsp tapenade

85g/3 oz black or green olives,
stoned and sliced

1 tbsp chopped fresh parsley,
to garnish

method

1 Cook the pasta in a large saucepan of boiling salted
water for about 4 minutes, or according to the packet
instructions, until tender but still firm to the bite.

2 Meanwhile, put the salt, oil, nutmeg, pepper, garlic,
tapenade and olives in another saucepan and heat
slowly but don't allow to boil. Cover and leave to stand
for 3–4 minutes.

3 Drain the pasta and return to the saucepan. Add the
olive sauce and heat gently for 1–2 minutes. Serve
immediately, garnished with chopped parsley.

mozzarella gnocchi

ingredients

serves 3-4

450 g/1 lb packet potato gnocchi
butter, for greasing
200 ml/7 fl oz double cream
225 g/8 oz firm mozzarella
  cheese, grated or chopped
salt and pepper

method

1 Cook the potato gnocchi in a large saucepan of boiling salted water for about 3 minutes, or according to the packet instructions.

2 Drain and put into the prepared baking dish.

3 Preheat the grill and grease a large baking dish. Season the cream with salt and pepper and drizzle over the gnocchi. Scatter over the cheese and cook under the grill for a few minutes until the top is browned and bubbling. Serve immediately.

desserts

nectarine crunch

ingredients

serves 3

4 nectarines
175 g/6 oz raisin and nut
  crunchy oat cereal
300 ml/10 fl oz low-fat
  natural yogurt
2 tbsp peach jam
2 tbsp peach nectar

method

1 Using a sharp knife, cut the nectarines in half, then remove and discard the stones. Chop the flesh into bite-sized pieces. Reserve a few pieces for decoration and put a few of the remaining pieces in the bottom of each of 3 sundae glasses. Put a layer of oat cereal in each glass, then drizzle over a little of the yogurt.

2 Put the jam and peach nectar in a bowl and stir together to mix. Add a few more nectarine pieces to the glasses and drizzle over a little of the jam mixture. Continue building up the layers in this way, finishing with a layer of yogurt and a sprinkling of oat cereal. Decorate with the reserved nectarine pieces and serve.

pan-fried apples or pears with maple syrup & walnuts

ingredients

serves 4

85 g/3 oz butter

4 firm apples or pears, peeled and cut into thick slices

3 tbsp maple syrup

2 tbsp brandy

4 tbsp walnuts

method

1 Melt half the butter in a frying pan and add half the apples or pears.

2 Cook for 2 minutes on each side until golden. Remove from the pan and cook the remaining fruit, then remove from the pan.

3 Add the remaining butter to the frying pan with the maple syrup, brandy and walnuts and bring to the boil. Remove from the heat.

4 Put the warm fruit into serving bowls and pour over the sauce. Serve.

fruit skewers

ingredients

serves 4

a selection of fruit, such as apricots,
    peaches, figs, strawberries,
    mangoes, pineapple, bananas,
    dates and papaya, prepared
    and cut into chunks
maple syrup
50 g/1¼ oz plain chocolate
    (minimum 70% cocoa solids),
    broken into chunks

method

1 Soak 4 wooden skewers in water for at least 30 minutes
    to prevent them from burning. Thread alternate pieces
    of fruit onto each skewer. Brush the fruit with a little
    maple syrup.

2 Put the chocolate in a heatproof bowl set over a
    saucepan of gently simmering water, ensuring that
    the bowl does not touch the water, and heat until the
    chocolate has melted.

3 Preheat the grill to high and line the grill pan with
    foil. Grill the fruit skewers for 3 minutes, or until
    caramelized. Serve drizzled with the melted chocolate.

grilled tropical fruits with spiced butter

ingredients

serves 4

115 g/4 oz unsalted butter

2 tbsp chopped stem ginger

½ tsp ground cinnamon

½ tsp grated nutmeg

2 tsp lemon juice

2 tsp icing sugar

4 bananas, halved

4 pineapple wedges

2 papaya, peeled, deseeded and sliced

1 mango, peeled, stoned and sliced

method

1 Cream the butter with the ginger, spices, lemon juice and icing sugar in a large bowl.

2 Spread half of the spicy butter mixture over the pieces of fruit.

3 Preheat the grill or barbecue. Place the fruit on the grill rack and grill for 2–3 minutes until they begin to caramelize.

4 Turn the fruit over, dot with the remaining spiced butter and grill until caramelized. Serve immediately.

orange & caramel bananas

ingredients

serves 4

115 g/4 oz granulated
    or caster sugar
1 tsp vanilla extract
finely grated zest and
    juice of 1 orange
4 bananas, peeled and
    thickly sliced
2 tbsp butter
ice cream, to serve

method

1 Put the sugar, vanilla extract and orange juice in a frying pan and heat gently until it forms a caramel.

2 Add the banana slices and cook, shaking the pan, for 1–2 minutes until they are coated with the caramel.

3 Add the butter to the pan and cook for a further 3 minutes, shaking the pan to coat the bananas.

4 Tip the bananas onto a serving plate and sprinkle with the orange zest. Serve hot with scoops of ice cream.

plums in spiced red wine

ingredients

serves 2–4

300 ml/10 fl oz red wine
3 heaped tbsp dark brown sugar
1 cinnamon stick, broken
4 cardamom pods, cracked
pinch of ground cloves
8 firm red plums, stoned
    and halved
4 tbsp crème fraîche, to serve

method

1 Put the red wine, sugar, cinnamon, cardamom and ground cloves in a saucepan and slowly bring to the boil, stirring until the sugar has dissolved completely.

2 Add the plums to the saucepan and cook gently for about 5 minutes.

3 Remove from the heat and leave to cool completely before serving with crème fraîche.

berry brûlées

ingredients

serves 4–6

450 g/1 lb berries, such as
     raspberries, strawberries,
     redcurrants and stoned
     cherries
300 ml/10 fl oz double cream
115 g/4 oz caster sugar

method

1 Divide the berries into 4–6 individual flameproof dishes
   or one large dish.

2 Whip the cream in a large bowl until thick but not stiff.

3 Spoon the whipped cream over the berries until they
   are evenly covered.

4 Preheat the grill to very hot. Sprinkle over the sugar to
   cover the cream completely and place under the grill,
   about 5–7.5 cm/2–3 inches from the heat source, for
   about 3 minutes, or until the sugar is bubbling and
   golden. Watch the sugar carefully – it will scorch if left
   too long.

cherry mascarpone creams

ingredients

serves 4

425 g/15 oz canned black
  cherries in syrup, stoned
1 tbsp rosewater
500 g/1 lb 2 oz mascarpone cheese
flaked toasted almonds or
  chopped pistachio nuts,
  to decorate

method

1 Drain the stoned cherries and reserve 2 tablespoons of the syrup.

2 Stir the rosewater into the reserved cherry syrup, then stir in the cherries.

3 Spoon into 4 serving dishes. Cover the cherries with the mascarpone and sprinkle with the almonds or pistachios. Leave to chill in the refrigerator until ready to serve.

white wine & honey syllabub

ingredients

serves 4–6

3 tbsp brandy
3 tbsp white wine
600 ml/1 pint double cream
6 tbsp clear honey
55 g/2 oz flaked almonds

method

1 Combine the brandy and white wine in a bowl.

2 Whip the cream in a large bowl until just thickened.

3 Add the honey to the cream and whip again for about 15 seconds.

4 Pour the brandy and wine mixture in a continuous stream onto the cream and honey mixture, whisking constantly until all the liquid is absorbed and the mixture forms soft peaks.

5 Spoon into serving dishes and leave to chill in the refrigerator for 2–3 hours.

6 Just before serving, scatter over the almonds.

mocha creams

ingredients

serves 2-4

12 marshmallows
125 ml/4 fl oz strong black coffee
55 g/2 oz plain chocolate, finely
chopped or grated
300 ml/10 fl oz double cream

method

1 Put the marshmallows in a saucepan with the coffee and half the chocolate. Heat gently until melted. Remove the pan from the heat.

2 Whip the cream in a large bowl until thick and softly peaking, then gently stir in the coffee mixture.

3 Spoon into 2-4 serving bowls or dishes and sprinkle with the remaining chocolate. Leave to chill in the refrigerator until ready to serve.

brown sugar mocha cream dessert

ingredients

serves 4–6

300 ml/10 fl oz double cream
1 tsp vanilla extract
85 g/3 oz fresh wholemeal
    breadcrumbs
85 g/3 oz dark brown sugar
1 tbsp instant coffee granules
2 tbsp cocoa powder
grated chocolate, to decorate

method

1 Whip the cream and vanilla extract together in a large bowl until thick and softly peaking.

2 Mix the breadcrumbs, sugar, coffee and cocoa powder together in another large bowl. Layer the breadcrumb mixture with the whipped cream in serving glasses, ending with whipped cream. Sprinkle with grated chocolate.

3 Cover tightly and leave to chill in the refrigerator until ready to serve.

jamaican cream

ingredients

serves 2

300 ml/10 fl oz double cream
2 tbsp light brown sugar
1 tbsp strong coffee or coffee
    liqueur
2 tbsp dark rum
2 ripe bananas
chocolate-covered coffee beans,
    to decorate

method

1 Whip the cream, sugar and coffee together in a large bowl until thick and softly peaking.

2 Gradually fold in the rum.

3 Peel and slice the bananas, then gently stir into the mixture.

4 Spoon into serving glasses or bowls and top with chocolate-covered coffee beans. Leave to chill in the refrigerator until ready to serve.

cheat's chocolate pots

ingredients

serves 4–6

140 g/5 oz good-quality plain
    chocolate (minimum 60%
    cocoa solids), broken into
    small pieces or chopped
400 ml/14 fl oz double cream
1 tsp vanilla extract

method

1 Melt the chocolate in a bowl set over a saucepan
    of simmering, not boiling, water, or melt in a glass
    or ceramic bowl in a microwave oven.

2 Remove the bowl from the pan or microwave and
    gradually stir in the cream and vanilla extract until the
    mixture is smooth.

3 Pour into small coffee cups or dishes and leave to chill
    in the refrigerator until ready to serve.

chocolate zabaglione

ingredients

serves 4

4 egg yolks
4 tbsp caster sugar
50 g/1¼ oz finely grated
    plain chocolate
125 ml/4 fl oz Marsala
cocoa powder, for dusting
amaretti biscuits, to serve

method

1 Put the egg yolks and sugar in a large heatproof bowl
    and whisk together using a hand-held electric whisk
    until very pale.

2 Fold the chocolate into the egg mixture. Gradually fold
    the Marsala into the chocolate mixture.

3 Set the bowl over a saucepan of gently simmering
    water and set the electric whisk on the lowest speed or
    use a balloon whisk. Cook gently, whisking constantly,
    until the mixture thickens; take care not to overcook
    or the mixture will curdle.

4 Spoon the hot mixture into warmed coffee cups
    and dust with cocoa powder. Serve the zabaglione
    as soon as possible so that it is warm, light and fluffy,
    accompanied by crunchy amaretti biscuits.

no-bake chocolate fudge cake

ingredients

serves 6–8

225 g/8 oz plain chocolate,
  broken into pieces
225 g/8 oz unsalted butter
3 tbsp black coffee
55 g/2 oz light brown sugar
few drops of vanilla extract
225 g/8 oz digestive biscuits,
  crushed
85 g/3 oz raisins
85 g/3 oz walnuts, chopped

method

1 Line a 450-g/1-lb loaf tin or a 20-cm/8-inch cake tin
  with greaseproof paper or non-stick baking paper. Melt
  the chocolate, butter, coffee, sugar and vanilla extract
  in a saucepan over a low heat.

2 Add in the crushed biscuits and the raisins and walnuts
  and stir well.

3 Spoon the mixture into the prepared loaf tin.

4 Leave to set, then chill in the refrigerator for 1–2 hours.
  Turn out and cut into thin slices to serve.

ginger baked alaskas

ingredients

serves 4

4 tbsp sultanas or raisins
3 tbsp dark rum or ginger wine
4 square slices ginger cake
4 scoops vanilla ice cream or rum
 and raisin ice cream
3 egg whites
175 g/6 oz granulated
 or caster sugar

method

1 Preheat the oven to 230°C/450°F/Gas Mark 8.

2 Mix the sultanas with the rum in a small bowl.

3 Place the cake slices well apart on a baking sheet and scatter a spoonful of the soaked sultanas on each slice.

4 Place a scoop of ice cream in the centre of each slice and place in the freezer.

5 Meanwhile, whisk the egg whites in a large grease-free bowl until soft peaks form then gradually whisk the sugar into the egg whites, a tablespoonful at a time, until the mixture forms stiff peaks.

6 Remove the ice cream-topped cake slices from the freezer and spoon the meringue over the ice cream. Spread to cover the ice cream completely.

7 Bake in the oven for about 5 minutes until starting to brown. Serve immediately.

chocolate banana sundae

ingredients

serves 4

150 ml/5 fl oz double cream
4 bananas
8–12 scoops good-quality vanilla
    ice cream
75 g/2¾ oz flaked or chopped
    almonds, toasted
grated or flaked chocolate,
    for sprinkling
4 fan wafers, to serve

chocolate sauce

55 g/2 oz plain chocolate,
    broken into small pieces
4 tbsp golden syrup
1 tbsp butter
1 tbsp brandy or dark rum
    (optional)

method

1 To make the chocolate sauce, put the chocolate, syrup and butter in a heatproof bowl set over a saucepan of barely simmering water. Heat, stirring, until melted and smooth. Remove the bowl from the heat and stir in the brandy, if using.

2 Whip the cream in a separate bowl until it is just holding its shape. Peel and slice the bananas. Put a scoop of ice cream in the bottom of each of 4 tall sundae dishes. Top with slices of banana, some chocolate sauce, a spoonful of the whipped cream and a generous sprinkling of nuts.

3 Repeat the layers, finishing with a good dollop of whipped cream, a sprinkling of nuts and a little grated chocolate. Serve with fan wafers.

index